We woke up one morning and found that our children had changed overnight.

Listen man, I tried to get to know a preppie once. But he said he already had a black friend.

Have you ever tasted their cooking? Have you ever put their cooking in your mouth?

I'd just like to see one of those preps last a day on a real job. That's what I'd like to see.

Last time one of them come through our parts was back in '47. Pappy used him for fertilizer.

Winners never prep. Preppies never win.

...my, I'm ...d!

Don't worry, baby. I won't let them get you.

This book is dork city.

SAVE AN ALLIGATOR SHOOT A PREPPIE™

A TERRORIST GUIDE

written by ROYCE FLIPPIN & DOUGLAS MCGRATH
drawings by FRANK WILLIAMS
produced by MICHAEL S. KATZ

A & W VISUAL LIBRARY
NEW YORK

Published by A & W Publishers, Inc.
95 Madison Avenue
New York, New York 10016

Designed by Frank Williams, Susan J. Aiello and Linda Wilson

TM registrations: The Button Man, Inc.
Chubby the Alligator drawn by Virginia M. Perkins

Library of Congress Number: 81-69742
ISBN: 0-89104-285-7

Dedicated to the boys and their couch in 10A Holder—RF
For Ratty—FW
Thesis—MSK

Printed in the United States of America

The premise of this book is simple. We think preppies are irritating. We believe Bermuda shorts look stupid, that socks were meant to be worn, and that no woman in her right mind would wear a hairband past her thirteenth birthday. We get nauseated at the sight of pink and green.

And now we're worried.

Preppies are multiplying. Suddenly they're everywhere: in the supermarkets buying cocktail clams; in the bars ordering G&T's; in the nightclubs, bouncing innocent dancers off the floor with their jitterbug spins. Our country is being swept away in a frenzy of button-downs and topsiders, and no one is safe from its dread grasp. You may find a prep playing on your son's Little League team, or sitting next to you in a public restaurant. Who knows—your sister may end up *marrying one*.

It's not ourselves we're concerned about. It's our children. We want them to grow up free, their little hands unspoiled by the touch of a squash racquet, their wrists unshackled by multi-colored watch bands. We want them to have the chance to think and dress for themselves, the American Way.

Unfortunately, preppies have forgotten their place—which is in Woods Hole and Groton, Connecticut, where they can tramp around in their weird duck boots and swap America's Cup stories without bothering the rest of us. Things have gotten out of hand. We're being overrun.

The solution is obvious. We must fight back as only rational, educated human beings can: with terror. Pure, unbridled terror—the kind that will blanch those St. Tropez tans, wipe the glaze of ennui from those half-opened eyes, and send each and every one of them whimpering back to the Norman Rockwell prints and restored furniture from whence they sprung.

That's where this book comes in: a thoughtful, step-by-step guide to terrorizing the khakis off those blond little monsters. We hope you read and enjoy it in the spirit of the old saying:

> *Conserva alligatorem—*
> *Caeda preppiem.*

Or, loosely translated,

> *Save an alligator—*
> *Shoot a preppie.*

The freedom of men and reptiles everywhere depends on it. Happy hunting.

The Authors

WHAT TO DO

some suggestions...

Send a preppie acquaintance
a shirt with an alligator on it.

Babysit small preppie children
and force them into
polyester playsuits.

Ask a preppie to play third base for your softball team.

Capture a preppie child
and make him take out the garbage.

Train your Doberman Pinscher to attack copies of *Town and Country*.

Break into the executive locker room at the Merrill Lynch VIP gym. Replace those baggy boxers with something more enticing.

Move to New Canaan, Connecticut.
Infiltrate the Junior League.
Gain their trust, and advance to the
rank of social chairman.

Announce you have
replaced Wednesday afternoon
tennis with something new.

Help a preppie family meet the Bar Harbour Express.

Put an aphrodisiac in the punch bowl at a Madeira School social.

Maroon two Groton boys on a desert island with a debutante and only one tuxedo.

Make a good impression on your college roommate. Do her hair the night of the Senior Prom.

Serve a Princeton man stew.

Buy a house in Greenwich
and add a personal touch
to the front yard.

Give Maine back to the Indians.

Get something fun for the rearview mirror of the family car.

Feed a preppie family Mexican food.

Feed a Mexican family preppie food.

Boycott Connecticut.

Get a "Buffy" doll to play with.

Visit a preppie's waterfront property in the Berkshires. Stock the pond with exotic fish.

Kidnap someone named Bitsy
and drop her off in the pant
suit department at Sears.

Inform a preppie that
his charging privileges at
L.L. Bean have been cancelled.

Make love to a preppie female with the lights on.

Make love to a preppie male
with the lights off.

Ask him to do it again.

It's Sunday at J.G. Melon's.
3:45 p.m. Early by prep standards.
Trip and Muff drag in for
brunch. They'd gone Borneo the
night before. The technicolor yawn
could come at any moment.
So brunch is key.
They order Bloodies.
"Sorry," you smile. "No
more tomato juice."

Crash a Main Line wedding with your uncle's Polish polka band.

Entertain youngsters at a preppie
birthday party with passages
from the *Communist Manifesto*.

Flash the Miss Porter's School
field hockey team.

Flash Miss Porter.

When inviting a prep school basketball team to play the Inner City All-Stars, observe the following musts and mustn'ts:

1) Be gentle when coaxing them out of the locker room. (The only other time they've been to Newark was to switch planes on the way to Aruba at Christmas.)

2) Don't point and laugh at their sweatsuits. They cost more than your gym.

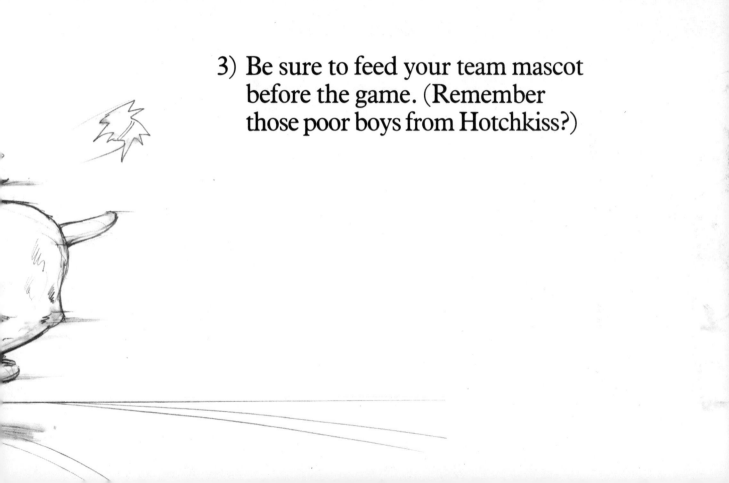

3) Be sure to feed your team mascot
before the game. (Remember
those poor boys from Hotchkiss?)

Post a provocative sign
halfway down the
upper slope at Sugarloaf.

Practice your racing turns at the Southampton Yacht Club Regatta.

Place a toaster in the Short Hills Country Club pool.

Arrive early at the
Harvard-Yale game. Park
your street van next to the
Brice-Worthington's tailgate party.
Leave the motor running.
Play Led Zeppelin's Greatest Hits.

Bury contact grenades midfield at the Longmeadow Polo Club.

Take a friend duck hunting.

Cut the rudder wires on the shell of the Dartmouth heavyweight crew.

Stage a native insurrection
in Bermuda during Spring break.

Breed giant lobsters off the shores of Nantucket.

Nuke the Vineyard.

Royce Flippin left Princeton University in 1980 with dreams of becoming a starving artist. He has since developed a dislike for tuna casserole and a deep craving for commercial success. Royce does not wear duck boots, topsiders or tweed jackets. He was last seen using an alligator shirt to clean up after pets and small children.

Doug McGrath graduated from the Choate school in 1976 and from Princeton U. in 1980. He was a member of the Ivy Club and used to summer in Edgartown on Martha's Vineyard. He did his senior thesis on Benedict Arnold, in whom he finds much to admire. He is now in hiding.

Though he lives daringly close to the Main Line in Philadelphia, Frank Williams has never been to the Devon Horse Show. The closest he's ever gotten to the Ivy Leagues was while attending art school two and one half miles from the U. of Penn. campus. Until recently, he thought L.L. Bean was something to eat.

Michael "Some Of My Best Friends Are Preppies" Katz started the whole anti-prep movement at Princeton at the tender age of 22. Having since worked his way up the anti-preppie corporate ladder from a two-button button man to a million-button button king, the newly gray-haired Katz eagerly looks forward to a long vacation.

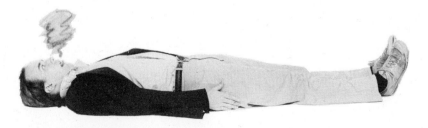

™